Contents

INTRODUCTION

Lime and Lemon are necessary fruits in your weekly ration!

What can you cook using Lime and Lemon? Cookies, cakes, pies… This is hardly a complete list. Try Sweet grazed chicken wings, Lemon Achiote grilled tofu, or Crispy Tilapia fingers under Lemon-Garlic mayonnaise and you will understand what I'm talking about. With this Lemon and Lime cook book you will fulfill all the needs for the recipes from main dishes to sweet desserts.

Lemons and limes are excellent not only as natural remedies for the previously mentioned conditions but also as ingredients in the kitchen, these fruits being quite versatile although, at first sight, it might seem lemons can only be used for preparing fruit juices and pies.

They contain not only vitamin C and P but also necessary amounts of calcium, potassium, vitamin B6, and fibers. Also, they're loaded with iron, magnesium, phosphorus, zinc and copper, thiamin and riboflavin, and they're inferior in sodium and fats.

PART1: LEMON RECIPES

1. Gingerbread Muffins with Lemon Glaze

It is not too spicy, and it tastes fantastic

Preparation time: 30 minutes

Yield: 3

Ingredients:

- 2¾ mugs generally useful flour

- two vast eggs

- 2½ teaspoons heating pop

- 1 glass sugar

- 1¾ mugs powdered sugar

- ½ teaspoon salt

- 1 1/3 mugs chilly water

- five tablespoons lemon juice

- 1½ tablespoons ground ginger

- One teaspoon ground cinnamon

- 1/8 teaspoon ground cloves

- ¾ container mellow enhanced molasses

Directions:

1. Preheat stove to 350°F. Utilizing a blender, mix the margarine and sugar, trailed by eggs and molasses.

2.   Add portion of the flour blend in with the general mish-mash, and beat. At that point embed the rest of the blend and continue beating until the point that the blend is very much mixed.

3.   Add chilly water and beat until the point when it winds up plainly one with the player.

4.   Grease 16 biscuit glasses with margarine, and scoop the player into them.

5.   Bake for 25 minutes or until the point when a toothpick embedded in the inside tells the truth. Give the biscuits a chance to cool for 10 minutes.

6.   To set up the coating, blend lemon squeeze, and powdered sugar, and make a smooth glue. Pour this over each of the biscuits equally.

7.   Serve warm, or at room temperature; it is totally up to you.

2. Date-Nut Bread with Lemon

It is a great dish for any occasion. It is very hearty.

Preparation time: 40 minutes

Yield: 3

Ingredients:

- 1½ glasses generally useful flour

- one vast egg

- ¾ glass bubbling water

- One teaspoon heating pop

- 1 container brilliant darker sugar

- ½ teaspoon salt

- ½ container unsalted margarine, at room temperature

- ½ teaspoon ground cinnamon

- 1½ teaspoons lemon peel

- three tablespoons new lemon juice

- 1 container slashed pecans

- 1 container slashed set dates

Directions:

1. Preheat the stove to 350°F.

2. In another bowl, beat spread to make it smooth.

3. Grease and flour a roll skillet. Add pecans to the hitter, and exchange it to the dish. Heat the batter for around 55 minutes.

4. Use your 'toothpick test' to decide if preparing is finished.

5. Use a blade to cut around the edges of the dish, and turn the bread out on a plate.

6.   Let the bread cool totally, before being served.

3. Lemon and Blueberry Buttermilk Pancakes

Everyone in your family will want to add this dish to your regular weekly meals.

Preparation time: 45 minutes

Yield: 3

Ingredients:

- 1 container generally useful flour

- one extensive egg

- One teaspoon preparing powder

- ½ teaspoon preparing pop

- Two tablespoons sugar

- A squeeze of salt

- two tablespoons spread, dissolved

- two tablespoons lemon get-up-and-go

- 1¼ mugs buttermilk

- 1-half quart blueberries

Directions:

1. Fold in the lemon get-up-and-go, and let the hitter sit for 10 minutes.

2. Lightly oil a cast-press frying pan with some margarine, and keep it on medium-low warmth. Pour ¼ measure of the hitter onto the iron for one flapjack.

3. Sprinkle a few blueberries over the hotcakes and cook for 2-3 minutes.

4. When the flapjacks turn brilliant dark colored on the edges, flip over and cook for 1 minute as it were.

5.   Repeat the procedure with the rest of the hitter.

4. Breakfast Cookies Lemon Vanilla Beans

Preparation time: 35 minutes

Yield: 3

Ingredients:

- ½ container almond flour

- ½ container coconut flour

- two eggs

- ½ teaspoon preparing pop

- ½ container coconut sugar

- ½ teaspoon ocean salt

- zest and juice of 1 lemon

- ½ container coconut oil

- beans from 1 vanilla unit

Directions:

1. Preheat your stove to 350°F. Take two tbsp. of batter and shape it into treats by moving it into a ball and push down.

2. Make treats out of all the mixture.

3. Line a heating sheet with dark colored paper, or oil it.

4. Place the treats on this sheet and heat for 15 minutes.

5. Let them cool totally before evacuating them.

5. Breakfast Pizza

This is not too spicy and it tastes wonderful.

Preparation time: 50 minutes

Yield: 3

Ingredients:

- one pizza batter

- lemon juice - 2 tablespoons

- Zest of 1 lemon

- 2 tbsp. liquefied spread

- 2 mugs mascarpone cheddar

- 1 tbsp. overwhelming cream

- four tbsp. cinnamon-sugar

- 2 containers blended berries

Directions:

1. Roll the batter out with a rolling-pin, and put it to the heating sheet.

2. Brush it with dissolved margarine, and sprinkle a half of the cinnamon-sugar on it.

3. Bake your pizza for 10-15 minutes, or until the point that it turns brilliant dark colored; let it cool.

4. In a bowl – blend cheddar, cream, lemon squeeze and get-up-and-go, and spread this blend over the pizza hull.

5. Sprinkle the rest of the cinnamon-sugar on top of the the pizza and toss some blended berries to finish everything.

6. Lemon Waffles

This dish is packed full of nutrients. You can now enjoy it any time of the year.

Preparation time: 30 minutes

Yield: 3

Ingredients:

- Zest and juice of 1 lemon

- ½ teaspoon lemon remove

- one egg

- 1¼ mugs skimmed drain

- 2 tablespoons icing sugar

- ½ teaspoon salt

- ½ teaspoon heating pop

- 1 tablespoon smooth fruit purée

- 1 tablespoon canola oil

Guidelines:

1. Before beginning set the waffle iron to medium warmth. At that point blend flour, icing sugar, heating pop and salt in an extensive bowl.

2. Separate egg white and yolk, and whisk the yolk with drain, fruit purée, lemon juice, pizzazz, lemon concentrate and canola oil.

3. Beat the egg white in a different bowl until the point that pinnacles are framed in it.

4. Add the egg white with a spatula for even circulation.

5. Grease the waffle press with canola oil, and cook the waffles for 20 minutes, or until brilliant dark colored.

7. Lemon & Poppy Seed Bread

For those who find the lemon flavor a little much, we add poppy seeds in this recipe. Perfect for breakfast. Have it with slices of fresh veggies like tomatoes, lettuce, and cucumber to have a controlled diet. The bread is so fresh that the texture isn't that hard, and is quite a tangy loaf.

Yields: **8 servings**

Preparation time: 20 minutes

Ingredients:

- 1 ½ cup plain flour
- ½ tsp baking powder
- 4 tbsp grated lemon zest
- 8 tbsp lemon juice
- ½ cup sugar
- 1 cup butter
- 1 ½ cup icing sugar
- ½ cup full cream milk
- Two whole eggs
- 5 tbsp poppy seeds
- ½ cup full cream

The method of Preparation:

1. Apply butter on a loaf tin.
2. Preheat the oven to 356F.
3. Beat the butter, icing sugar and poppy seeds till creamy using a food processor.
4. Add the eggs one by one while beating simultaneously.
5. Add the milk and cream and fold in the flour gently.
6. Use a spatula to mix the loaf mixture.
7. Make a syrup in a saucepan using the sugar, lemon juice, and lemon zest.
8. Boil for 2-3 minutes.
9. Pour over the baked loaf when it's still hot.

Nutritional value Per Serving:

Calories 145.5;

Total Fat 3.6 g;

Cholesterol 0 mg;

Sodium 56.6 mg;

Potassium 345.1 mg;

Total Carbohydrates 27.4 g;

Fiber 2.9 g;

Sugar 3.5 g;

Protein 3.1 g

8. Lemon Rose Pancakes

Add the tanginess of lemons to your breakfast with our lemon rose pancakes. The essence of rose will just fill your house, and your children will be rushing to the table to get a bite of this beautiful, luscious dessert.

Yields: **8 servings**

Preparation time: 25 minutes

Ingredients:

- Rose syrup
- 3 eggs
- 2 cups full cream milk
- 5 tbsp butter
- A pinch of salt
- Six rose petals
- One tsp vanilla essence
- One tsp almond essence
- 5 tbsp sunflower oil
- 2 tbsp icing sugar
- 2 tbsp grated lemon zest
- 1 tbsp baking soda
- 1 cup whipped cream

The method of Preparation:

1. Leaving aside the rose syrup, combine all the ingredients in a large bowl.

2. Keep it aside for 30 minutes.
3. Cook on both sides until golden yellow in color.
4. Serve with rose syrup and cold whipped cream.

Nutritional value Per Serving:

Calories 145

Total Fat 8.6 g;

Cholesterol 0 mg;

Sodium 71.6 mg;

Potassium 467.1 mg;

Total Carbohydrates 16.4 g;

Fiber 2.9 g;

Sugar 3.5 g;

Protein 1.1 g

9. Lemon & Coconut Cake

This delicious, flavorful cake is the sure forerunner. Coconuts add richness and lemons balance the sweetness. Make it, take a bite, and I bet you, in few days you'll be baking much more batches of this beautiful cake. Can't get better then lemon and coconut, what you still waiting for? Get started!

Yields: **8 servings**

Preparation time: 30 minutes

Ingredients:

- 2 eggs
- 2 tbsp lemon juice
- 1 cup milk
- 1 ½ cup butter
- 1 ½ cups sugar
- 4 cups plain flour
- One tsp baking powder
- ½ tsp salt
- 1 tbsp grated lemon zest
- 5 tbsp icing sugar
- 3 tbsp fresh lemon juice
- 5 tbsp desiccated coconut

The method of Preparation:
1. Preheat oven to 275 F.
2. Spray cooking spray on a loaf tin and keep it aside.
3. In a large bowl, beat the sugar and butter till creamy in texture.
4. Add the salt and salt and fold well.
5. Stir in the lemon zest and desiccated coconut

6. Mix the remaining lemon juice and icing sugar and make it slightly loose so that it could spread well on the cake
7. Pour it over the cake and sprinkle the desiccated coconut over it.

Nutritional value Per Serving:

Calories 151.5;

 Total Fat 4.6 g;

Cholesterol 0 mg;

Sodium 71.6 mg;

 Potassium 441.1 mg;

Total Carbohydrates 26.4 g;

Fiber 3.9 g;

Sugar 5.5 g;

Protein 2.1 g

Cookie Recipes

10. Basic Lemon Cookie

This recipe uses a cake mix for a fast, easy, scrumptious treat.

Preparation time: 35 minutes

Yield: 3

Ingredients:

- 2 eggs

- Three teaspoons lemon juice

- 1/3 glass vegetable oil

- One lemon cake blend

- 1/3 glass confectioner's sugar

Directions:

1. Preheat broiler to 375 degrees F

2. Mix eggs, oil, lemon squeeze and cake blend

3. Drop little chunks of batter into confectioner's sugar and move around to coat - Place on a treat sheet and prepare for 5 to 10 minutes

11. Lemon Tea Cookies

These cookies will be a hit with your family, friends or party guests. They're perfect for serving with tea.

Preparation time: 40 minutes

Yield: 3

Ingredients:
- 2 containers flour

- 1/2 teaspoons lemon get-up-and-go

- Four sticks and 1/6 measure of room temperature spread

- 2 2/3 containers powdered confectioner's sugar

- 1/4 container lemon juice (crisply pressed is ideal)

- 1/2 teaspoon vanilla concentrate

- 1/2 mugs cornstarch

Directions:

1. Preheat stove to 350 degrees F

2. Beat four sticks of spread until smooth

3. Mix in 2/3 glass powdered sugar until feathery

4. Beat in vanilla concentrate and one teaspoon lemon get-up-and-go - Add cornstarch and flour and blend well

5. Roll batter into balls or utilize a treat scoop

6. Place bundles of batter on treat plate

7. Bake 15 minutes

Icing Procedure:

1.   Combine 1/4 container lemon juice, 1/6 glass spread, 2 mugs powdered sugar and 1/2 teaspoon lemon get-up-and-go - If the icing is too thick, include more lemon juice

12. Soft Lemon Cookies

These sweet and tangy cookies have an awesome balance of texture. For even more lemony goodness, make a glaze of drizzling on top using 2 tbsp. of lemon juice and a cup of powdered sugar.

Preparation time: 30 minutes
Yield: 3
Ingredients:

- 1 egg

- One egg yolk

- One tablespoon cornstarch

- 1/2 teaspoon salt

- 2 glasses and two tablespoons flour

- 1/4 glasses sugar

- 1/2 teaspoon heating pop

- 3/4 glass diminished margarine

- Two tablespoons crisp lemon juice

- Zest of 2 lemons

- 1/2 teaspoon vanilla concentrate

Directions:

1. Preheat stove to 350 degrees F

2. Whisk flour, preparing pop, cornstarch, and salt together

3. In isolated bowl, blend spread, lemon pizzazz, and sugar together on medium-fast for around 3 minutes

4. Mixture ought to be soft

5. Bake 8 to 12 minutes

Cake Recipes

13. Quick and Easy Lemon Cake

This cake is simple and satisfying with a light lemon flavor.

Preparation time: 40 minutes
Yield: 3
Ingredients:

1 container sugar

- -Two teaspoons lemon get-up-and-go

- -3/4 container drain

- -1/2 teaspoon salt

- -1 egg

- 1/2 teaspoons preparing powder

- 1/4 containers flour

- -One teaspoon lemon juice

- -1/4 container softened margarine or spread

Directions:

1. Preheat stove to 350 degrees F

2. Mix sugar, preparing powder, salt and flour in a 8x8 inch heating container - Mix lemon pizzazz and egg together with fork

3. Pour into container with margarine

4. Add drain and blend well

5. Bake 30 to 35 minutes

6. Cool and include icing and lemon get-up-and-go top

14. Lemon Sponge Cake

This lemon sponge cake is moist and savory.

Preparation time: 45 minutes

Yield: 3

Ingredients:

- White sugar - 1 cup
- Milk -1/2 cup
- 2 eggs
- One tbsp. lemon juice
- 1 1/2 cups self-rising flour
- One stick of melted butter

Instructions

1. Mix 1 cup sugar with butter
2. Beat eggs
3. Add eggs with one tbsp. lemon juice to the butter and sugar mixture Mix in milk and flour
4. Bake 1 hour at 325 degrees F

15. Lemon Pound Cake

This cake is versatile. Enjoy it by itself, with fruit or with your favorite ice cream.

Preparation time: 35 minutes
Yield: 3

Ingredients:
- White sugar - 1 cups
- 1/2 cup milk
- 2 eggs
- One tbsp. lemon juice
- 1 1/2 cups self-rising flour
- One stick of melted butter

Instructions
5. Mix butter and 1 cup sugar
6. Beat eggs
7. Add eggs and one tablespoon lemon juice to the butter and sugar mixture Mix in flour and milk
8. Bake for 1 hour at 325 degrees F

16. Lemon Achiote Grilled Tofu

This is a great appetizer recipe that will please the kids and the rest of the family.

Preparation time: 30 minutes

Yield: 3

Ingredients:

- 12 ounces additional firm tofu

- Two tbsp. achiote powder

- ¼ tbsp. cayenne pepper

- One tbsp. darker sugar

- ½ tsp. salt

- 1/3 glass lemon juice

- Three peeled garlic cloves

Directions:

1. Mix cayenne pepper, achiote powder and sugar. Spray salt over peeled garlic, and cut it up into a glue.

2. Add this and lemon juice to the achiote blend, and mix. Cover the tofu with the achiote blend, and place it in a preparing dish.

3. Refrigerate it for 60 minutes.

4. On a medium hot flame broil, cook the tofu and spread some a greater amount of the achiote blend to finish everything.

5. When you see the flame broil lines on the base of the tofu, cook the opposite side similarly.

6. Once flame broiled, expel from warmth and serve it the way you need.

17. Parmesan Crusted Tilapia

This is a great appetizer recipe that will please the kids and the rest of the family.

Preparation time: 40 minutes

Yields: 3

Ingredients

- Four tilapia filets

- One tablespoon lemon juice

- ¼ container breadcrumbs

- Two teaspoons garlic powder

- ½ teaspoon salt

- ½ teaspoon dark pepper

- One teaspoon olive oil

- ¼ container parmesan cheddar, ground

- One tablespoon Italian flavoring

Directions:

1.   On a plate, blend breadcrumbs, cheddar, garlic powder, and flavoring. On another plate, pour lemon juice and, one by one, put a filet in the drain and sprinkle a squeeze of genuine salt, dark pepper, and garlic powder.

2.   Flip the filet and sprinkle flavoring on the opposite side.

3.   Dip each filet in the cheddar blend and coat it pleasantly.

4.   Grease a heating dish with some olive oil, and place the filets on it.

5.   Pour a little lemon squeeze on the filets and delicately cover them with oil.

6.   Bake them at 425°F for 20 minutes, or until the point that the edges are dark colored.

18. Crispy Tilapia Fingers under the Lemon-Garlic Mayonnaise

This is a great appetizer recipe that will please the kids and the rest of the family.

Preparation time: 40 minutes

Yield: 3

Ingredients:

- 2 lbs. tilapia filets

- 1 container generally useful flour

- 3 eggs

- Two tablespoons olive oil

- One teaspoon dark pepper

- Lemon wedges

- 1 container mayonnaise

- One clove garlic

- Two tbsp. lemon juice

- One teaspoon salt

- 2 containers breadcrumbs

Directions:

1. Put flour in a blending dish, beaten eggs in another, and breadcrumbs in the third. Cut the filets into little fingers by cutting them into half and afterward part every half corner to corner.

2. Coat fish fingers with flour, shaking to evacuate overabundance. At that point coat them uniformly with egg, and afterward with the breadcrumbs.

3. Turn a few times in the two dishes for covering. Put the fingers on an aluminum thwart covered heating sheet and add salt and pepper.

4. Heat olive oil in a non-stick skillet over medium warmth.

5. Place the fish fingers in, to such an extent that they are not swarmed. Cook for 2-3 minutes until the point that the base is brilliant dark colored, at that point flip the fingers and broil similarly.

6. Transfer them to a plate secured with paper towels to deplete the overabundance oil.

7. To set up the lemon-garlic mayonnaise, blend mayonnaise, garlic and lemon squeeze in a bowl, and spread the glue over the fingers.

19. Lemony Chickpea Stir-fry

This is a great appetizer recipe that will please the kids and the rest of the family.

Preparation time: 40 minutes

Yield: 3

Ingredients:

- Two tablespoons additional virgin olive oil

- 1 glass kale, cleaved

- 1 teaspoon ocean salt

- 1 glass cooked chickpeas

- 2 little zucchini, cleaved

- 1 little onion

- 8 ounces additional firm tofu

Guidelines:

1. Heat 1 tablespoon of oil in a skillet over medium-high warmth, and include a squeeze of salt, onion and chickpeas.

2. Cook until the point when the chickpeas are dried up and brilliant. Blend in the tofu and cook for 2 minutes, until the point when it is warmed.

3. Add kale and cook for one more moment. Exchange the substance of the skillet onto a huge plate.

4. Using a similar skillet, warm the rest of the oil, and cook the zucchini for 2-3 minutes.

5. Sprinkle lemon squeeze and get-up-and-go, and serve.

20. Honey-Glazed Lemon-Roasted Chicken

This is a great appetizer recipe that will please the kids and the rest of the family.

Preparation time: 50 minutes

Yield: 3

Ingredients:

- 7 lbs. broiling chicken, flushed and tapped dry

- ¼ container nectar

- Juice of 6 lemons

- A couple of sprigs of thyme

Directions:

1. Preheat the stove to 450°F.

2. Place thyme sprigs in the hole of the chicken. Place the chicken, bosom side down, on a simmering skillet, and prepare for 15 minutes, at that point bring down the temperature to 375°F, and cook for 45 minutes.

3. Coat the chicken with nectar.

4. Cook at 350°F for 50-55 minutes, sometimes brushing the chicken.

PART 2: LIME RECIPES

21. Savory Watching Your Weight Key Lime Pie

It is the perfect recipe for anyone who is looking to please their family or a crowd.

Preparation time: 30 minutes

Yield: Makes 8 Serv.

Ingredients:

- 1 (8 ounces) holder sans fat whipped besting

- 2 (6 ounces) yoghurt, preferably "key lime pie"

Directions:

1. Mix in yogurt with a wire whisk.

2. Put in covering.

3. Leave it in a refrigerator for no less than 2 h.

22. Ambrosial Frozen Key Lime Pie

You will love this recipe, and it will remind you of what your grandma used to make

Preparation time: 45 minutes
Yield: Makes 8 Servings

Ingredients:

- Four egg yolks

- 1 (5 ounces) can sweeten consolidated drain

- 1/4 glass key lime juice

- Four egg whites

- 1/4 glass white sugar

- Prepared graham saltine outside layer

Guidelines:

1.   In an expansive bowl, smash yolks to light and fleecy.

2.   Blend in lime juice.

3.   Place in fridge while whipping whites.

4.   Gently overlap whites into yolk blend. Fill outside layer and stop. Serve solidified.

23. Heavenly Easy Pezzy Key Lime Pie

Your family will enjoy this dish, and it will become your new family favorite

Preparation time: 45 minutes
Yield: Makes 2 Pies

Ingredients:

- Two graham saltine pie hull

- 1 can solidify limeade focus

- 1 container Cool Whip

Directions:

1.   Combine Sweetened consolidated drain, limeade and cool whip in a blending dish.

2.   Stir until completely blended.

3.   Pour into two graham saltine outsides.

4.   Let chill.

5.   The filling will wind up noticeably firmer when refrigerated.

24. Nectarous Two-Layer Key Lime Pie

This dish is hearty and quick to throw together. This recipe is perfect for anyone who is always on the go.

Preparation time: 40 minutes

Yield: Makes 8 Servings

Ingredients:

- One teaspoon vanilla concentrate

- 2 spoons Butter

- 3 spoons Sugar

- 5 spoons Granola

Directions:

1. Preheat stove to 350 F.

2. Transfer granola into a blending dish.

3. Add wafer morsels, softened spread, and sugar.

4. Remove from stove and let chill totally.

5.   Turn the stove down to 300 F.

6.   Put into the pie hull.

7.   Leave it to reach the room temperature.

8.   Pour over the cooled prepared layer.

25. Tasteful Catahoula's Key Lime Pie

Your whole family will love it and will ask you to make it more often.

Preparation time: 40 minutes

Yield: Makes 6-8 Servings

Ingredients:

- Two substantial eggs

- Two limes, get-up-and-go

- 1 container Baking flour

- 3 spoons baking pop

Directions:

1. Preheat stove to 350 degrees.

2. Thoroughly blend all fixings.

3. Remove from stove.

4. Pour into pie covering.

5.   Evacuate and let cool.

6.   Refrigerate until prepared to serve.

26. Pleasurable Frozen Key Lime Pie

The dish is creamy and once you have it, you will crave it.

Preparation time: 45 minutes
Yield: Makes 8 Servings

Ingredients:

- Four egg yolks

- 1/4 container key lime juice

- Four egg whites

- 1/4 container white sugar

- 1 (9 inches) arranged graham wafer hull

Guidelines:

1.	In a substantial bowl, beat yolks until light and feathery.

2.	Blend in lime juice.

3.	Place in fridge while whipping whites.

4.	In an expansive glass or metal blending dish, beat egg whites until frothy.

5.	Gently crease whites into yolk blend.

6.	Pour into outside layer and stop. Serve solidified.

27. Dramatic Refreshing Lime Pie

You will absolutely go crazy when you get your first bite.

Preparation time: 35 minutes

Yield: 8 Servings

Ingredients:

- One pack of unflavored gelatin

- 1⁄2 glass icy water

- 1⁄2 glass bubbling water

- 3 (8 ounce) containers sans sugar sans fat lemon yogurt

- 1 1⁄2 mugs light whipped beating

- One shortbread pie covering (8 inches)

Guidelines:

1. In a separate bowl, break down lime gelatin in bubbling water; blend in unflavored gelatin until broke up.

2. Put it to refrigerator for 10 minutes or until thickened.

3. Stir in yoghurt.

4. Cool until somewhat set.

5. Fold the whipped besting.

6. Put into covering.

7. Let it cool down until firm.

28. Titillating No Egg Key Lime Pie

This is an awesome appetizer recipe that will please your kids and the rest of the family.

Preparation time: 30 minutes
Yield: 8 Servings

Ingredients:

- 1 (14 ounces) can sweeten consolidated drain

- 8 ounces mellowed cream cheddar

- 2⁄3 container key lime juice

- 1⁄2 tsp. vanilla

- One graham saltine pie outside

- Whipped beating

- Lime cut, for decor

Guidelines:

1. In a blender, blend dense drain, cream cheddar, and lime juice.

2. Add vanilla and mix until blended through.

3. Put into graham saltine hull.

4. Add whipped garnish to the highest point of the pie.

5.   Leave in refrigerator for 3-4 hours before serving.

6.   Decorate best of the pie with lime slices.

29. Tender and Tangy "Baked" Yams with Coconut Lime "Butter."

This dish is hearty and quick to throw together. This recipe is perfect for anyone who is always on the go.

Yields: 8 servings

Preparation time: 30 minutes

Ingredients:

- Six small garnet yams, unpeeled (or very small sweet potatoes)
- Two tablespoons (30 g) coconut oil, melted (or melted unsalted butter)
- One tablespoon (15 ml) freshly squeezed lime juice
- Wash the sweet potatoes clean and do not chuck them dry.

The Method of preparation

1. Slice all sweet potatoes into thin pieces
2. Heat coconut oil in a pan for 2 minutes
3. Bake the sweet potatoes until it is cooked in both sides
4. Make syrup in a saucepan using the sugar and lime juice.
5. Pour over the baked sweet potato loaves

30. Sweet and Sassy Thai-Glazed Baked Wings

Now you can enjoy them all together in a soup that is just as delicious as each individual food.

Yields: **8 servings**

Preparation time: 20 minutes

Ingredients:

- Three tablespoons (45 ml) sesame oil
- Three tablespoons (45 ml) low-sodium tamari (or low-sodium soy sauce)
- 3 tablespoons (45 ml) fresh-squeezed lime juice four cloves garlic, minced
- 2 pounds (905 g)
- chicken wings
- (about 12) 1/3 cup (92 g)
- Thai sweet chili sauce
- Two tablespoons (28 ml)
- unseasoned brown rice vinegar
- 1/4 cup
- (60 ml) low-sodium chicken broth (or water)
- One teaspoon Sucanat, palm sugar or xylitol
- 2 teaspoons

- (4 g) minced fresh ginger
- Two teaspoons (5.4 g) kudzu plus
- one tablespoon (15 ml) cold chicken broth or water (or 11/2 teaspoons
- 4 g, cornstarch and simmer a little longer to cook off starchy flavor)
- 1/4 cup (25 g) sliced scallion

The method of preparation

1. In a glass storage container, mix the oil, tamari, lime juice, and garlic. Place the prepared wings in the bowl and toss gently to coat.
2. Oven should be preheated to 350°F (180°C).
3. Dissolve the kudzu in the broth or water and put to the boiling sauce. Take it away from the heat and cool slightly.
4. Stir in the scallion and cilantro and glaze the cooked wings to taste just before serving.

CONCLUSION

Thank you for downloading this cookbook.

Thanks to their ingredients, these fruits increase the rate of urination, which means they also work as natural diuretics. Fruits help in detoxifying the liver, liquefy the bile and assist in the removal of toxins. By adding lemons to your daily menu, it's easier to keep constipation and other digestive issues away.

Vitamin C contained in fruits helps the body absorb calcium more efficiently, and this prevents osteoporosis. Also, fruits contribute to building stronger and healthier bones in children during their intrauterine life. Therefore these fruits should be incorporated in their daily diet by pregnant women.

 People suffering from low energy levels can benefit from the ingredients provided by lemons, fruits that revitalize the body and fight against adrenal fatigue. The adrenal glands are involved in regulating energy levels as well as in the production of certain hormones linked with stress, moodiness, and nervousness.

By working on the adrenal glands, lemons also control the body's level of hydration, keeping away the unpleasant effects of dehydration: mood swings, headaches, irritability, concentration and memory problems, impaired vision, dizziness, skin and mouth dryness and so on.

By purifying the blood, fruits contribute to a better delivery of oxygen to cells. Also, they prevent a cough and colds, which can alter breathing, and provide quick relief from asthma symptoms.

Some other health benefits of lemons include insomnia prevention, a healthier brain and nervous system, and improved cognitive performance and an overall state of well-being.

Fruits provide 22 anti-cancer compounds so they can be effective in preventing certain types of cancer as well. These fruits prevent travel sickness, help in treating nausea and vomiting, prevent rheumatic disorders and reduce the harmful effects of radiations.

Lemons and lime are excellent not only as natural remedies for the previously mentioned conditions but also as ingredients in the kitchen, these fruits being quite versatile although, at first sight, it might seem lemons can only be used for preparing fruit juices and pies.

They contain not only vitamin C and P but also necessary amounts of calcium, potassium, vitamin B6, and fibers. Also, they're loaded with iron, magnesium, phosphorus, zinc and copper, thiamin and riboflavin, and they're inferior in sodium and fats.